unapologetic

A Coloring Journal for Black Women with Prompts for Self-Discovery, Awareness and Creativity

By
Nina Foxx (+ You)

Book Design by Beryl Jennings

ISBN: 979-8-9867706-0-4 (Paperback)

ISBN:979-8-9867706-1-1 (Hardcover)

ISBN: (Spiral)

Published by Clever Vixen Media, LLC

Introduction

Before March of 2020, I was a sometime yogi, taking an occasional yoga class when it fit into my exercise routine. I enjoyed yoga as an exercise and vowed that one day, I would take a yoga teacher training to deepen my own practice. At that time, in my head, yoga was too slow. It forced me to slow down and be introspective in a way I was not ready for, instead I opted for what I considered to be more hard-core, old-fashioned exercise like hard cardio and fast classes. These were too hard to let me think about anything other than what I was doing, leaving no room to actual turn inward and feel what I was doing or what was going on with my body or mind.

Like many people, when the pandemic started, I needed to find something to let off steam and to fill up the two extra hours a day I no longer had to spend commuting. All gyms closed and all fitness competitions were cancelled. Online yoga teacher training became approved as life moved to virtual. The universe was speaking to me. I was offered a scholarship to become a yoga teacher. Now was the time for my yoga teacher training.

Although I was taking the training for my own benefit, or so I told myself, I was still required to teach a number of hours to complete my program. I needed real students, so I conscripted family and friends. I was not prepared for the response, not from myself or others. I believed that family and friends would roll their eyes and humor me; instead, they embraced the classes I offered with open arms. Before this time, many did not feel welcome in western yoga classes, and being remote on Zoom offered some feeling of safety. They felt as if the yoga spaces they'd previously been exposed to were often not inclusive of varying ages, sizes and shapes, especially the shapes that brown and Black people most often came in. Yoga, as they had experienced it, was geared towards people who were already fit, wore size two clothes, and who could afford expensive studio memberships.

Instead of encouraging people to bend into shapes their bodies didn't want to take naturally, my classes encouraged people to explore where they were physically and take gradual, gentle and healthy steps towards wellness, using movements that would help their functional health while counteracting some of the negative by-products of things we need to do as ordinary people, such as sitting at a desk all day and staring at a computer.

Part of the yogic process as I was learning it and teaching to others is a self-exploration. We set intentions for class, focusing on the things we want to work on during that class and maybe the rest of the day or week. Prior to my training, yoga was just a physical workout for me. Over the hundreds of hours of training and practice, a lightbulb turned on for me. Yoga was also a workout of the mind. I pinned the intentions I chose in my classes to traditional yoga principles with the everyday Black woman in mind and wrapped that in a culturally welcoming and inclusive environment. Soon, I found students telling others about the intentions of our classes. This had become yoga off the mat.

We often spend so much time doing and working for others that we don't set aside time to work on things for ourselves. I designed Unapologetic: A Coloring Journal for Black Women with Prompts for Self-Discovery, Awareness and Creativity as an extension of the inward focus that our yoga practice taught me. The Journal is broken down into sections, with exercises, quotes by Black and Indigenous women, and images to color. All are designed to help the reader with work that they might otherwise neglect to do for themselves.

How to use this book

There is no right way to use this book. It is organized into sections to help guide your introspection and creativity. Each section begins with a short introduction, followed by a quote that was chosen to help frame your thinking for the exercises to follow. Before the writing prompts, you will find a coloring page to stimulate mindfulness. These can be colored, or if you are a painter, have at it with some watercolors! The next section includes a series of writing prompts related to the main theme. You can choose all of them or some of them, but they are designed for self-exploration. Finally, there are creative exercises, designed to be done off the page so you can take what you've learned about yourself and your world a little further into a multi-dimensional activity, making space for you embrace all that you are —unapologetically.

Purpose

Have you ever stopped to think about the question of "Why am I here?" Everything in your life has had a purpose. It has brought you to where you are now.

What are the most important recent events in your life?

_____

_____

_____

_____

_____

_____

_____

_____

_____

_____

_____

_____

_____

_____

_____

_____

How do these events relate to what you perceive as your life's purpose and/or meaning?

What people are important in your life?

_____

_____

_____

_____

_____

_____

_____

_____

_____

_____

_____

_____

_____

_____

_____

How do these people impact your life purpose?

_____

_____

_____

_____

_____

_____

_____

_____

_____

_____

_____

_____

_____

_____

_____

_____

Are there people in your life detrimental to your life's purpose? Who? What's keeping you from ending the connection?

_____

_____

_____

_____

_____

_____

_____

_____

_____

_____

_____

_____

_____

_____

_____

_____

_____

_____

Creative Activities

1. Make a list of your goals for the next year.

2. Under each goal, make a list of ways to reach that goal.

_____

_____

_____

_____

_____

_____

_____

_____

_____

_____

_____

_____

_____

_____

_____

joy

today
I CHOOSE
joy

We are so often bogged down in "grinding", trying to move forward towards some grand goal, that we overlook the smaller things in our lives that are important and make us feel good. We forget to experience the things that are here right now. Achieving is good, but achieving just for the sense of saying you have done this is exhausting. As Black women, we have been taught to overachieve. This relentless pursuit of achievement often leaves the steps in between a blur, and we forget to slow down and incorporate some joy in our lives by appreciating the small steps in between.

"Be with life as it is unfolding." -Nina Foxx

Make a list of ten things that make you feel comforted,
present, inspired, and just plain good. How can make time
for these joyful experiences in your life?

_____

_____

_____

_____

_____

_____

_____

_____

_____

_____

_____

_____

_____

_____

_____

_____

Who brings joy to your life?

_____

_____

_____

_____

_____

_____

_____

_____

_____

_____

_____

_____

_____

_____

_____

_____

What food brings you joy? Why is that? Explore the
memories that are connected to it.

_____

_____

_____

_____

_____

_____

_____

_____

_____

_____

_____

_____

_____

_____

_____

_____

What prevents you from experiencing joy?

_____

_____

_____

_____

_____

_____

_____

_____

_____

_____

_____

_____

_____

_____

_____

_____

Creative Activities

Fill a box with pieces of paper with the activities that bring you joy. Pull out two slips a week and surprise yourself with that activity. Alternatively, you and your significant other can take turns filling the box with activities.

Self-Care

Self-care is more than massages and pedicures from the trip to the mall. Self-care also includes such things as taking care of yourself mentally and emotionally and is about knowing your boundaries and knowing the things that make you feel good. As your awareness of these things increases, so will your kindness to yourself.

"Caring for myself is not self-indulgence, it is self-preservation, and that is an act of political warfare."
—— *Audre Lorde*

What boundaries can you set to enable you to feel less rushed and have more time for yourself?

_____

_____

_____

_____

_____

_____

_____

_____

_____

_____

_____

_____

_____

_____

_____

_____

Part of setting boundaries is being able to say no to things that will add unnecessary stress and complexity to your day. What are three ways that you can say no when people ask you to do things?

_____

_____

_____

_____

_____

_____

_____

_____

_____

_____

_____

_____

_____

_____

_____

_____

What is a choice you can make this week that is based on your needs?

_____

_____

_____

_____

_____

_____

_____

_____

_____

_____

_____

_____

_____

_____

_____

_____

Make a list of five things that make you feel good.

_____

_____

_____

_____

_____

_____

_____

_____

_____

_____

_____

_____

_____

_____

_____

_____

What helps you slow down?

Creative Activities

Put on a lip color that makes you feel confident, even if you are just staying home.

Put on a song you love that makes you dance and go at it.

Unplug from your email and social media for at least an hour.

love

When was the last time you looked at your relationships? They change over time, and in times of uncertainty, when so many things feel as if they are out of control, the one thing we can control is to whom we give emotional access. Boundaries in relationships are a sign that the relationships are valued.

"No person is your friend who demands your silence or denies your right to grow." — Alice Walker

What relationships in your life make you feel seen? Why?

_____

_____

_____

_____

_____

_____

_____

_____

_____

_____

_____

_____

_____

_____

_____

_____

_____

What are your deal breakers in a friendship? In a relationship?

What is your ideal size in a social circle? Why?

_____

_____

_____

_____

_____

_____

_____

_____

_____

_____

_____

_____

_____

_____

_____

_____

What are some ways you can communicate your needs to others in a relationship?

_____

_____

_____

_____

_____

_____

_____

_____

_____

_____

_____

_____

_____

_____

_____

_____

_____

Creative Exercises

Show love by baking something for a friend or neighbor, or offering to pick up groceries for a neighbor.

Connect with a trusted friend or loved one. Don't just text. Try and old-fashioned phone call, or plan a lunch date, just because.

Motivation

Many of us have deep desires, goals and a driving force to live a meaningful life. Often, there are steps that stand in the way of the things we want that don't feel so desirable but are a means to an end.

A"I get angry about things, then go on and work."
-Toni Morrison

What are three things in your life that you do regularly but have to force yourself to get done? What do these things have in common?

_____

_____

_____

_____

_____

_____

_____

_____

_____

_____

_____

_____

_____

_____

_____

_____

How do they make you feel in your body, and while you are doing them?

_____

_____

_____

_____

_____

_____

_____

_____

_____

_____

_____

_____

_____

_____

_____

_____

What goals have you achieved in the past that you were particularly proud of? How did this make you feel?

_____

_____

_____

_____

_____

_____

_____

_____

_____

_____

_____

_____

_____

_____

_____

What are some techniques or practices you can use to help you push through the unpleasant to get to the things you want to achieve?

_____

_____

_____

_____

_____

_____

_____

_____

_____

_____

_____

_____

_____

_____

_____

_____

Creative Activities

Motivate your friends by inviting them to a coloring party. They could each bring a copy of this book or another book they'd like to color and you could pick a section of the book you'd like to discuss.

Grace

To give yourself grace means giving yourself permission to forgive your mistakes, your lapses in judgement and hurtful behavior. No one is perfect, and making mistakes often provides opportunity for growth and learning and can lead to better well-being and emotional relationships.

"Mistakes don't define me. They teach me." -unknown

What does forgiveness mean to you?

Is forgiveness hard for you? Why or Why not?

Have you been punishing yourself? What about? Why?

_____

_____

_____

_____

_____

_____

_____

_____

_____

_____

_____

_____

_____

_____

What are three things from your past that you need to forgive yourself for to move forward? Write in as much detail as possible.

_____
_____
_____
_____
_____
_____
_____
_____
_____
_____
_____
_____
_____
_____
_____
_____
_____

Think about one of the things from the previous question.
What three things did you learn from the experience?

_____

_____

_____

_____

_____

_____

_____

_____

_____

_____

_____

_____

_____

_____

Creative Activities

Take fifteen minutes to feel your feelings. Take deep breaths through your nose while you do this, breathing in for four counts and out for six. Now, give yourself grace.

Faith

Inherent in the idea of faith is the understanding that nothing that you do in your life, you do alone, and that in the grand scheme of things, you are not, by far, the most important being in the universe. You exist with, around and adjacent to others, and we are all here for some reason that is usually unbeknownst to us. Faith and worship are inextricably connected. Faith leads to worship, and that does not necessarily mean "church." Worship can push you into your destiny and cleanse you of your past.

"Without faith, nothing is possible. With it, nothing is impossible." — Mary McLeod Bethune

What do you do to connect with what's bigger than you and why is that important?

Do you feel a sense of calling on your life? Where do you believe it stems from?

_____

_____

_____

_____

_____

_____

_____

_____

_____

_____

_____

_____

_____

_____

_____

_____

What do you feel called to do? How will you ensure that this thing, whatever it is, gets a larger slice of your "pie"?

_____

_____

_____

_____

_____

_____

_____

_____

_____

_____

_____

_____

_____

_____

_____

_____

How do you feel called to help others? How will you put this into action? How will you make room for this in your "pie"?

_____
_____
_____
_____
_____
_____
_____
_____
_____
_____
_____
_____
_____
_____
_____
_____
_____

Creative Activities

The things that you direct most of your energy towards are the things you worship. Draw a circle in your journal or on a Piece of paper. Divide it by percentages, labelling it for where you exert most of your energy, e.g. family, work, hobby, etc. Notice what gets the most of your pie.

Does it look like what you expected? What do you want to change, and why? Did you add yourself/self-care to that pie? Now, write down three ways you plan to work towards "Right-sizing" your pie. Remember to pay devote some time to the diamonds inside yourself.

Take fifteen minutes to pray or meditate, whichever resonates with you.

Gratitude

The odds of you coming into being were 1 in 400 trillion. It is easy to forget this and get bogged down by the negatives that we are surrounded with daily from such places as news and social media, and the things that we don't have, forgetting to be grateful for the good things in our lives.

"We learned about gratitude and humility — that so many people had a hand in our success, from the teachers who inspired us to the janitors who kept our school clean... and we were taught to value everyone's contribution and treat everyone with respect."
— Michelle Obama

What is a mistake that you've made that ultimately led to something good in your life?

_____

_____

_____

_____

_____

_____

_____

_____

_____

_____

_____

_____

_____

_____

_____

_____

Write about someone that you have never met that improved your life in some way.

_____

_____

_____

_____

_____

_____

_____

_____

_____

_____

_____

_____

_____

_____

_____

_____

_____

What are three simple things in your life that you are grateful for?

_____

_____

_____

_____

_____

_____

_____

_____

_____

_____

_____

_____

_____

_____

_____

_____

Write about a happy memory.

Open your phone and find a photo that you like. What are you grateful for in this photo?

_____

_____

_____

_____

_____

_____

_____

_____

_____

_____

_____

_____

_____

_____

_____

_____

_____

_____

Creative Activities

For the next five people you see, find something to compliment them on when you interact with them. Compliments are a way of making others feel appreciated, and they help us to focus on what we are grateful for in others. People will often return the favor and help us see what we should be grateful for about ourselves.

Resilience

Inherent in the idea of resilience is the idea of bouncing back from adversity, but we don't always have to bounce back to where we were. Instead, we can also use resilience to pull ourselves up. The pandemic left many people struggling; one of the keys to feeling resilient is the idea that one has control over the things and circumstances in our life, and many of us felt as if that control was stripped away.

"Wanna Fly, got to give up the shit that weighs you down."
-Toni Morrison, Song of Solomon

How will you use your resilience to move forward in your life?

_____

_____

_____

_____

_____

_____

_____

_____

_____

_____

_____

_____

_____

_____

_____

_____

What is one thing that you are nervous about? What can you do to move past it and grow from it?

What things can you sacrifice in the short term in order to reach your long-term goals? Make a quit list, listing five of these things.

_____
_____
_____
_____
_____
_____
_____
_____
_____
_____
_____
_____
_____
_____
_____

What was one of the happiest moments you had in the past year? Where was it? Why were you happy? How did you feel?

_____

_____

_____

_____

_____

_____

_____

_____

_____

_____

_____

_____

_____

_____

_____

Envision a happy moment you want to have in the next year. What does that look like? How will you feel?

Creative Activities

Our breath is one thing that we can absolutely control, and focusing on it helps bring us back to the matter at hand in times of stress. Deep breathing sends a message to your brain to calm down and that you are okay. Find a quiet place and sit quietly with your eyes close. Begin to focus on your breath, breathing in through your nose and out through your mouth. Breathe deeply, feeling your chest rise and your lungs fill, then exhale slowly, emptying them all the way out. Repeat for ten minutes.

Mindfulness

Mindfulness is the act of paying attention on purpose so that we can be more aware of ourselves and our feelings or actions and how we interact in the world around us. Everyone has gifts, even though they may not recognize them. It is far easier to see the beauty and gifts in others than it is to realize these same qualities in ourselves. We must examine our actions and the things that are beautiful about ourselves to bring these things into full awareness and recognize areas for self-improvement.

"Learn to be quiet enough to hear the genuine within yourself- Marian Wright Edelman

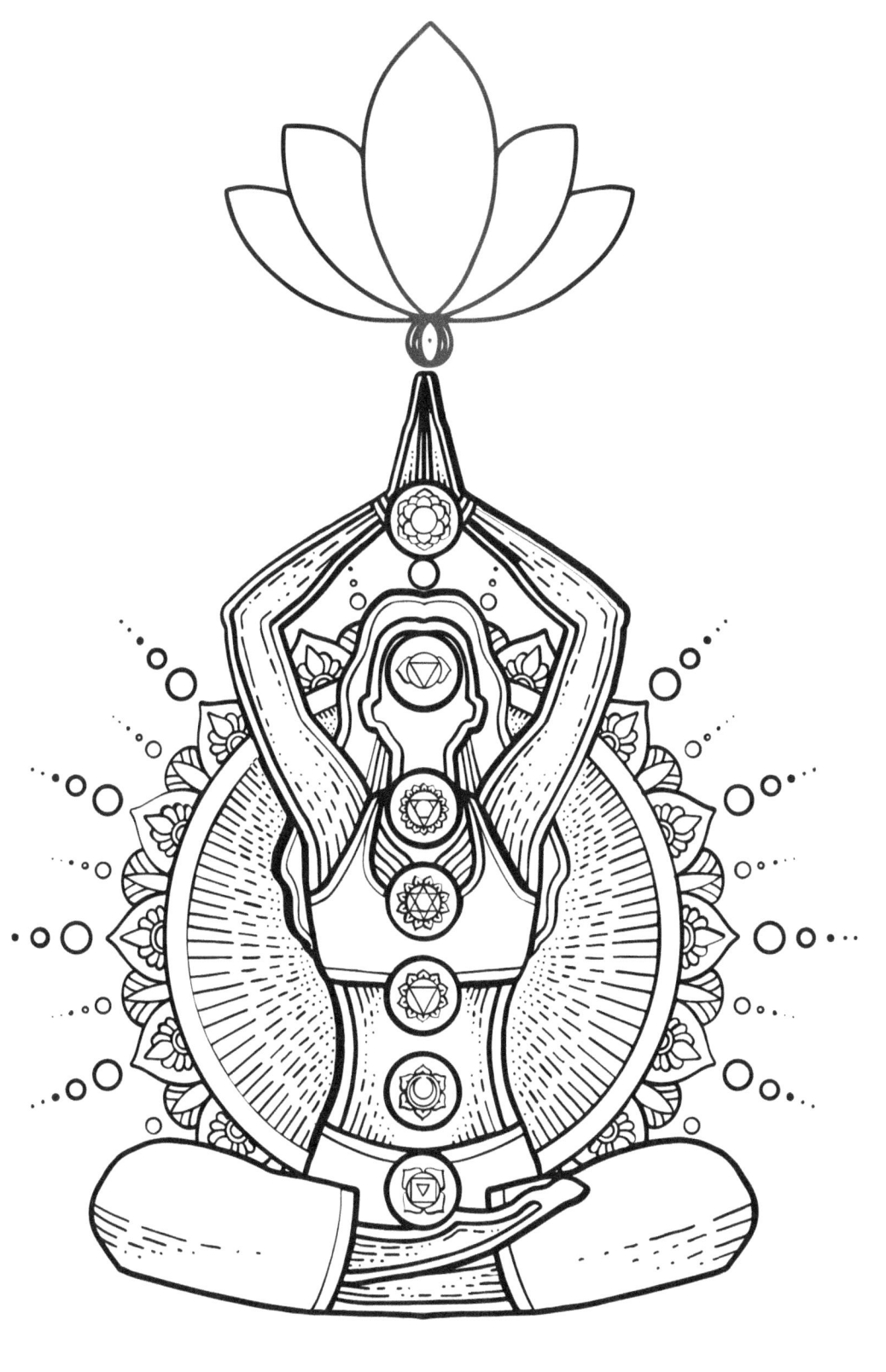

What are your top two good qualities and skills or gifts?
What can you do to best express these things?

_____

_____

_____

_____

_____

_____

_____

_____

_____

_____

_____

_____

_____

_____

_____

_____

Sit quietly for three minutes. Inhale deeply through your nose, and then exhale slowly, emptying your lungs totally. What are the sensations you notice when you do this? Write about these and the feelings and memories they trigger.

_____
_____
_____
_____
_____
_____
_____
_____
_____
_____
_____
_____
_____
_____
_____
_____
_____

Choose a routine thing that you have to do inside your home like cleaning the bathroom or doing the laundry or dishes. Pay attention to every single part of the task. What do you notice?

_____

_____

_____

_____

_____

_____

_____

_____

_____

_____

_____

_____

_____

_____

_____

_____

Think about last holiday season. What were some times where you tempted to spend money necessarily, but didn't? How did you feel then?

In your next conversation with another person, take the time to really focus on the words and notice their actions and body movements. Leave your phone face down and minimize distractions from electronics. How did you show them, with your actions, words and movements that you were fully engaged? Write about this and what you noticed during the interaction.

_____

_____

_____

_____

_____

_____

_____

_____

_____

_____

_____

Creative Exercises

1. Get an adult jigsaw puzzle and spend an afternoon or evening working on it.

2. Get your favorite beverage and drink it mindfully. Listen to the sound it makes as you pour it into the glass. As you drink, listen to the sounds you make as you swallow. Pat attention to how you feel as you do it.